MEDITATION AND THE TRANSFORMATION OF MIND

Windhorse Publications

Meditation and the Transformation of Mind

A System of Meditation, by Vessantara, was previously published in the Friends of the Western Buddhist Order Newsletter no. 42, Spring 1979.

Conquering the Hindrances, by Kamalashila, A Hair-Raising Experience, by Nagabodhi, and Meditation and Action, by Subhuti, were previously published in the Friends of the Western Buddhist Order Newsletter no.58, Summer 1983.

Windhorse Publications
136 Renfield Street
Glasgow G2 3AU

© Windhorse Publications 1986

Printed by Ink Print & Design
136 Renfield Street
Glasgow, G2 3AU

Cover illustration by Dharmachari Aloka

ISBN 0 904766 25 X

CONTENTS

CONTENTS

EDITOR'S PREFACE

The four short essays contained in this booklet originally appeared in issues 42 and 58 of *The Friends of the Western Buddhist Order Newsletter.* As editor of the Newsletter, I have often been pleased to hear how popular these articles were, and how helpful they have proved to 'generations' of new Friends.

Since those original issues of the Newsletter went out of print, a number of class and retreat leaders in our Movement have asked whether we could arrange to have these articles reprinted in some easily accessible form, so that they might remain available to those taking their first steps in the dimension of meditation.

This we have now done, with a few small revisions, and the result is this booklet. While it does not pretend to say even a fraction of all that can be said about the vast subject of meditation, I hope that the information and advice to be found in its pages will continue to offer some timely encouragement, and a warm invitation, to those making their first acquaintance with the 'direct method'.

Dharmachari Nagabodhi

A SYSTEM OF MEDITATION
By Dharmachari Vessantara

(1) Why Meditation?

'The object of meditation is to transform oneself, not to have good meditations.' This quotation from Sangharakshita's *Poems, Sayings and Reflections* sums up the whole purpose of meditation within the Buddhist context. Meditation is not an end in itself, not a flight into escapist fantasies, nor even into the states of joy or bliss — if these are viewed as ends in themselves. It is a tool for transformation, and must therefore be seen in the context of activities such as community living, right livelihood projects, study groups, artistic activities; those pursuits which further our 'development' as individuals — what Sangharakshita, interpreting traditional Buddhist teaching into Western parlance, calls the 'Higher Evolution' of Man. What is the essence of this 'Higher Evolution', and why does meditation play such an important part in promoting it?

Whereas Man's evolution to date has taken place primarily on the biological and physiological levels, his 'Higher Evolution' must be what, for want of a better term, we could call 'spiritual'; i.e. the process of self-transformation of which the Higher Evolution consists is a development of ever higher levels of consciousness. These higher levels of consciousness are characterized by the presence of what Buddhism calls 'skilful mental states' and the absence of 'unskilful states'. Skilful states of mind are those based on contentment, loving kindness, and clarity; unskilful states are rooted in their opposites: craving, aversion, and ignorance. Spiritual practices are therefore disciplines which promote these skilful mental states (which are naturally enjoyable and truly satisfying), and which root out unskilful mental states (which are unsatisfying and often painful). The word 'meditation' can be used to denote dwelling in skilful mental states, or the practice — especially in sitting meditation — of specific methods to achieve this. In this article we are mainly concerned with the latter of these connotations, but always bearing in mind that the practice of sitting meditation is not an end in itself, but an attempt to generate and maintain skilful mental states in ideal conditions. Such states gradually 'overspill' into our entire life, until we experience them as an uninterrupted flow under all circumstances and at all times.

In the Friends of the Western Buddhist Order (FWBO), great stress is laid on meditation practice because it is the *direct* method of cultivating skilful mental states. In meditation we work directly 'on the mind with the mind'. All other methods, such as Hatha Yoga or artistic appreciation, are indirect — transmitted to the mind through the five senses — and thus, whilst they are very useful, and should find a place in any balanced programme of spiritual development, they do not have the power and immediacy of meditation. All FWBO centres include meditation classes as an integral part of their programme, and in all our communities the day begins with a period of meditation.

(2) The Process of Transformation

Meditation, as we have seen, fosters a process of self-transformation. Whilst different individuals' experience of meditation may vary, because the basic 'structure' of the mind is the same in all human beings we can chart some common features of the process which may be found in anyone who meditates consistently. The process falls broadly into three stages, which we call the stages of concentration, absorption, and insight.

When people begin to practise meditation, they soon become aware that it is difficult to remain focussed on the object of their meditation. It is as if they are not one unified individual but more like a 'bundle of selves'. One 'self' has decided to meditate, another may want a cup of tea, another may want to think about a play he saw last night, and so on. Often, it seems, there is an endless parade of different selves, all pulling the mind in different directions. Consequently, one's energy is scattered and dissipated among the conflicting demands of these competing selves. The first stage of meditation is, therefore, the development of concentration — which integrates all these energies into a harmonious flow, 'binds together' this 'bundle of selves', and produces one overall direction for them. When all the 'selves' or energies of which we are consciously aware have been harmonized and focussed on the object of our meditation, then we have achieved what we call 'horizontal integration'.

This 'horizontal integration' of the elements of our conscious mind is relatively easy to achieve — at least for short periods — even for a beginner. But the part of the mind which falls within conscious awareness is only the tip of the iceberg. The next task is to achieve 'vertical integration' by harmonizing the energies of both the conscious and unconscious minds. This is much harder to achieve than 'horizontal integration'; it takes time for the process of meditation to 'filter through' and begin to affect the depths and heights of the mind. When this 'vertical integration' is achieved we will have started to go beyond the stage of concentration, and to embark on the stages of absorption.

The 'absorption' we refer to here is an absorption in higher states of consciousness than those which we usually experience. These higher states can be broadly schematized into four successively higher levels, although we must remember that each level develops out of the 'fullness' of its predecessor, and to talk of 'levels' at all is to impose a rigid structure on a natural and dynamic process. We can call the first stage the level of 'integration'. Here we have achieved both horizontal and vertical integration of our energies, we feel happy and emotionally buoyant, and there is a complete absence of neurotic mental chatter, although there may still be some discursive mental activity. This we could say is a truly human level.

If we can develop this level fully, we begin to reach the level of 'inspiration', and feel ourselves to be in contact with a fresh spring of creative energy. This is a level of true artistic creativity. From this level onwards, discursive mental activity has died away. This does not mean that the mind is left blank or dead. Rather, there is a state of tremendously heightened awareness, and what could be termed a 'thrilling peace', which is far more deeply satisfying than our more normal mental tick-over.

Out of the plenitude of this level there arises the stage of 'permeation'. At this level we experience the energy not so much as bubbling up 'within' us, but as permeating our whole being. Our whole mind and our environment as well seem to be transfigured by the higher level of consciousness. This we could term a level of mystical experience.

Lastly, we can go even beyond this to the level of 'radiation'. At this level our state of mind is so positive that we cannot be affected by anything negative whatsoever. Indeed so powerful is our concentration, and so strongly positive are our emotions that they can affect our external environment, even acting at a distance in a supranormal way. So this level is traditionally the one on which we might develop various so-called supernatural powers. We could characterize it as a magical level.

By the time we achieve this level, our process of self-transformation has been carried a long way. This level of experience is in fact regarded by some religious traditions as the goal of spiritual life. But the distinctive contribution of the Buddhist tradition has been to recognize that even at this stage the process of self-transformation has not been taken far enough. Indeed, someone who comes thus far, and yet who makes no further effort, can gradually lose everything which has been gained, because the underlying causes of unhappy states of mind have not been removed. It is like cutting off tenacious weeds at ground level: their roots remain, and if one ceases to be vigilant they will grow back, often with surprising speed. It is only with the development of insight into Reality that one finally uproots the causes of one's existential suffering or dissatisfaction for ever. So, with a mind refined, powerfully focussed, and purified of all subjective distortion by our previous practice, we turn to the contemplation of Reality itself, using as a guide one of the traditional formulations of the Buddha's teaching on the nature of Reality.

Usually, when people try to answer existential questions such as 'Who am I?' they cannot get very far, because their thinking is scattered and unconcentrated. At best they come up with purely intellectual answers. But the mind of the meditator who has reached the stage of developing insight is really concentrated, like a powerful searchlight penetrating into darkness; his emotional state is completely positive so he is prepared to welcome Truth, whatever it may be.

The development of insight is no cosy settling-down into comfortable ideas; it is an overpowering experience which transforms our whole being. At first it may come in flashes, but as we continue practising, these flashes of insight become more prolonged, until finally our minds will dwell permanently in the radiant state of illumination, marked by the complete flowering of the qualities of Wisdom and Compassion, which is called Enlightenment, the goal of the spiritual life.

(3) The 'System' of Meditation

Having gained some understanding of the purpose of meditation, and of the main stages through which we can pass if we commit ourselves to its practice, it is time to turn to a discussion of specific methods. For meditation is not something vague and woolly, not a matter of closing our eyes and going into a dream; rather, it comprises a systematic development of positive states of mind. We must therefore begin by learning a specific method or technique.

Within the Buddhist tradition there are literally thousands of different meditation practices. All are designed to produce specific effects such as the eradication of a particular negative emotion and the cultivation of its opposite; some are recommended for people of particular personality-types; all have been tried and tested by meditators for centuries — and in some cases for at least two thousand years, so we know they work! Within the FWBO and the Western Buddhist Order there are certain methods which we have found to be particularly valuable, and these form the elements of what we could describe as a 'system of meditation'.

When someone comes along to an introductory class at one of our Centres, they will learn two basic methods: the Mindfulness of Breathing and the *metta bhavana*. The Mindfulness of Breathing is the most fundamental of all Buddhist meditations. It is a concentration exercise, as well as an 'antidote' to restlessness, anxiety, and worry. As most of our Centres are in busy conurbations it is essential that people should begin by learning to calm and settle their minds to some extent. However, the main effect which this practice has is one of integration. It helps people to harmonize and bring together all their different energies, and to focus them; to bring from the chaos of different 'selves' one overriding 'self'. This is essential because the process of development which is initiated when one takes up meditation requires commitment: it requires every scrap of energy which we possess to bring about a radical change in our whole level of being and consciousness. So in learning to concentrate we learn to conserve energy, not to dissipate it, and we develop a sense of selfhood, of individuality, which provides the motivation to practise without being constantly side-tracked by other preoccupations.

At the same time that we teach the Mindfulness of Breathing, we also teach the *metta bhavana* — a Pali term which can be roughly translated as 'the development of universal friendliness, or goodwill'. This practice springs from the understanding that Man is not just a rational animal; indeed his thinking processes often provide little more than rationalizations for feelings. If the process of self-transformation is to be more than an intellectual fantasy we must work to transform our whole emotional nature. Through this practice we gradually develop feelings of warmth, friendliness, and well-wishing for ourselves (for charity begins at home), for those who are close to us, and by degrees, to everything that lives. This feeling is not exclusive, not based on what people do for us, nor merely aimed towards particular personality-types which we happen to find agreeable. Metta, when fully developed, is a totally inclusive feeling, felt equally towards all, and springing from our own emotional fullness irrespective of external circumstances.

Many people find it takes them some while to generate any strong feeling of metta, but as they gradually succeed it is no exaggeration to say that their experience of themselves and the world is transformed. Many people in the modern world feel cut off from their feelings, or feel that their emotions are totally conditional upon the pleasant or unpleasant experiences which they have. Many religions are quite strong on moral exhortations, to love and good-neighbourliness. But exhortations, of themselves, have little effect. Through the systematic practice of this meditation, however, it is possible actually to transform our emotions, to turn depression into joy, and hatred into love.

These two practices form the foundation of all further growth. They complement and reinforce one another so that, gradually, both our awareness and concentration and our positive feelings become stronger, and overspill more and more from our practice of sitting meditation into all our activities, until our whole life becomes 'meditation' in the wider sense.

However, even when we have concentrated our energy and developed powerful positive emotions, there is still much further to go. We have not yet developed insight into Reality, and consequently the causes of suffering and negative states have not been uprooted. So, at this stage, we can take up one of a number of practices designed to help us develop insight. The most commonly used of these practices within the Western Buddhist Order (for such practices are by and large confined to those who have made a definite commitment to the spiritual life) is called the Six Element Practice. Through this practice we analyse all the elements both physical and mental which go to make up what we think of as 'ourselves'. In so doing, we see that there is no part of us which we own as a 'personal possession', everything is in process of change.

For example, we see that the physical elements which go to make up our bodies are only 'borrowed' from the physical universe; our bodies are changing all the time. One day we shall die, and those elements will 'return' to the Universe. So this insight into Reality has the force of a kind of death, a 'spiritual death', in which the idea we have of ourself as an unchanging 'self', however positive and aware, is given up. But this 'spiritual death' is not the end, for one 'dies' in order to be 'reborn', transfigured into a shining being, an Enlightened being.

So the final major body of meditations practised within

the Order is that of the visualization of Buddhas and Bodhisattvas. In these practices we customarily begin by visualizing an infinite expanse of clear blue sky; this could be said to symbolize the boundless openness, the complete freedom, and infinite potentiality which the death of our 'lower self', with all its limited conceptions, has permitted.

Then, in the midst of the blue sky, we visualize the appearance of a shining figure, radiant and colourful, with a smiling, serene countenance, holding emblems which represent different qualities of Enlightenment, such as Wisdom, Compassion, or Energy. As we contemplate this figure we gradually 'absorb' more and more of its qualities, we become more and more identified with it, until we feel completely at one with it. Enlightenment is no longer a distant goal, it is a living experience.

It is hard in so short an article to do justice to so central a topic as meditation. But I hope the reader will have gathered that meditation is dynamic and systematic, that it is not identified purely with sitting meditation as an end in itself, but aims at the constant experience of skilful mental states whatever we may be engaged in; and that it is above all a great adventure, the greatest possible adventure that we can undertake: a process of self-transformation which leads from concentration, through higher states of consciousness, to Insight, and culminates in Enlightenment.

This can never be a selfish endeavour, and the more one progresses the greater is one's desire to *share* what one has experienced. All our Centres offer classes, led by members of the Western Buddhist Order who are experienced in meditation. You can come along just to achieve some peace of mind, or you can come determined to gain Enlightenment. The main thing is that you come, and practise.

CONQUERING THE HINDRANCES

By Dharmachari Kamalashila

How did primitive man make fire? By twirling a fire-stick, a pointed stick of hard wood which bores into a dry board of softer wood. By revolving such a stick between the palms of one's hands, for a long time, the point will get hot. Tiny pieces of dry kindling are added to the bore-hole, and as one keeps twirling the stick, eventually they get hot too. With a careful breath, they start to glow. The glow, with patience, is coaxed, with more of the precious dry matter, until at last a small red tongue of fire crackles out into the dry leaves. The main point that any master fire maker would make to a novice in the art is this: 'You really have to mean business! You really have to start the way you mean to go on. What is more, you have to have everything ready — dry kindling, twigs, wood — and you must be prepared to really work. It might take quite a long time to get even a little glow; and throughout that whole time, there is no possibility of slackening off — you have to keep going!' If he had heard of the Dharma, he might have said, 'It's just like meditation'. The art of making fire and the art of meditation require the same approach.

It was this very example of fire making that occurred to Chi-i, the great meditation teacher of sixth century China, when he was trying to find words to express what meditation is really like. To meditate, we first need to know what we want. Then we need to start — and keep going without stopping until we have what we want! Chi-i says,

'[This] . . . is characterized by an earnest and zestful spirit; It means to keep the precepts with a persevering eagerness of spirit; it means to give up the five hindrances, and to persevere with our practice with wholehearted zeal both in the evening and in the early morning. If you were trying to get fire from a twirling stick you would not expect to be successful if you did it intermittently; you must practise with increasing effort until the fire comes. So you must seek Enlightenment with the same earnest zeal.'

Meditation requires a lot of energy, a lot of application, a lot of persistence and stamina. Looking at it in another way, it is a bit like a battle: to win a battle you need a high resolve, and you need to know your objectives. Our objectives in this case are higher, happier states of consciousness, the *jhanas*. Between us and the *jhanas* are a few enemies to be conquered: the five gross hindrances (*nirvarana*).

We will deal with each of these in turn. First of all, let's remind ourselves of what the five hindrances are. The first is 'Desire for Sense Experience'. In meditation the senses are not in operation. But we find it difficult let them go: we still hanker after sense experience. Therefore we don't get away from them, and we don't get into a state of concentration. What we do is fantasize, using our imagination to play with images and memories of sense-impressions that are already in our minds. We have sex fantasies, food fantasies, fantasies about people and places — anything that feeds our desire for sense experience — all kinds of things that keep us on a relatively superficial level of experience, and prevent us from meditating. Basically, emotionally, we don't want to meditate.

How can we rid ourselves of this hindrance? First and foremost by recognizing that it is a hindrance. Otherwise we will not appreciate that anything is wrong. But there is something wrong — we could be meditating! And real meditation is much more enjoyable than fantasy.

The second hindrance, Hatred, is basically the same thing. The mind is hooked onto an object that it is unwilling to leave alone; but this time the object is one that causes us pain. Strange creatures aren't we? We don't want to meditate because that would mean letting go the painful fantasy we are attached to! So here again, our mental activity is mainly fantasy — this time about what we'd like to do, what we'd like to say to the person concerned; and we also reflect on their mountainous faults that apparently only we can see.

We may find it hard to admit, but this kind of fantasy is very painful, very self-destructive, and it gets us nowhere. To get beyond this hindrance, we have to recognize it as a hindrance first of all. Then, and only then, will we be in a position to use some means, such as the *metta bhavana* practice, to dissolve it.

These first two hindrances make up a pair, being both concerned with craving. The next two make up another pair which is concerned with very different modes of energy.

Restlessness and Anxiety, the third hindrance, has two components. Restlessness, the first, is the inability to settle down. The mind is rushing fitfully hither and thither. We have no particular track, no purpose: there is just energy more or less out of control. Anxiety, the second component, is irrational anxiety; it isn't as though there were anything concrete to worry about — but we feel anxious, tense, worried, on edge, so this too prevents us from finding, or even from looking for, the peace and calm of meditation. We are far too much on the surface of things, in a scatty, speedy, and anxious state of mind.

Again the antidote, the way out of this hindrance, is first to recognize that it is a hindrance; and then, in whatever way we can, to try to become calmer and more concentrated. Paradoxically, the most effective means of dealing with this hindrance is meditation itself, so we should redouble our efforts, and our resolve, to concentrate on what we are meant to be doing.

The opposite mode of energy is the hindrance of Sloth and Torpor: dullness, heaviness, stagnation, blockage of both bodily and mental energy. Sloth is mental dullness; torpor is physical heaviness: the sort of feeling we get after a very substantial meal. Naturally, this gives us a rather unpromising start for any sort of meditation. To get rid of it we first have to recognize it as a hindrance, which will not be easy. Recognizing it as a hindrance has implications! It implies that we have to do something about it, and sloth-and-torpor will resist this. What happens with all the hindrances is that we tend to identify ourselves with that state of mind — so we have always to remind ourselves that there are higher states just beyond our sight.

Doubt and Indecision, the fifth hindrance, stands on its own. Perhaps it underlies all the others, since it is basically through lack of confidence in our meditation — and in ourselves — that the other hindrances arise. We are only limited, little humans after all, we think. We doubt that Enlightenment is a real possibility for us. Having only got so far with our meditation, we doubt whether there really is any more. And of course, as soon as we limit our expectations in this way, further progress is made impossible.

Indecision is the other component of this basic hindrance — we don't make the decision to get on with the meditation, because any decision, once made, requires acting upon. We shrink from action because we have no confidence in ourselves; we remain stuck fast in indecision. So we really must do something about doubt and indecision. First recognizing it for what it is: a hindrance. Then we ask ourselves, 'Do I want to develop or not? Is it possible for me to develop or not?' We must then answer, 'Yes, I do want to develop. Yes, it is possible for me to develop!' In this way we'll become more confident; and on that basis we'll decide to get on with it; and we will have got beyond the hindrance of doubt.

Now we have been through all five we will have seen that the most effective means of conquering the hindrances is *recognition*: seeing that the hindrance is a hindrance, and deciding to move out of it. And because we tend to identify with the mental states we happen to be in at a particular time, this will require imagination and confidence.

To move out of the hindrances requires that we find a method which works in our own case. Each person's mind is unique and only very general guidelines can be given for finding a method. The following sequence of four traditional antidotes might give us some ideas. Firstly there is cultivation of the opposite tendency — e.g. *metta* (loving kindness) to counter hatred; secondly, we can consider the consequences of allowing the hindrance to take us over completely (which might have a sobering effect); thirdly, 'passive resistance' — allowing the hindrance to come and go as it will, but giving it no particular attention (which would keep it going); fourthly, the last resort is suppression, forcing it out of the mind.

In meditation we should be looking all the time to see whether we are really meditating or not. There must be an element of purposiveness, of knowing why we are doing what we are doing, knowing what we want and whether we are achieving it: we must check up on ourselves continually. This should be our strategy. Without some form of strategy, we will never be able to conquer the hindrances. Whether it is the *metta bhavana*, a visualization, or any other practice we are doing, this approach is necessary. It is just like the art of making fire — you can't afford to take your attention away for a moment, or everything is lost and you have to start again. You can only stop for a little while when there's a great blaze going.

A HAIR-RAISING EXPERIENCE

By Dharmachari Nagabodhi

As an expert bath attendant, or a bath attendant's apprentice, puts soap powder into a dish, soaks it with water, mixes and dissolves it in such a manner that its foam is completely permeated, saturated within and without with moisture, leaving none over, even so the monk suffuses, pervades, fills, and permeates his body with the pleasure and joy arising from seclusion, and there is nothing in all his body untouched by the pleasure and joy arising from seclusion . . .

As a lake with a subterranean spring, into which there flows no rivulet from East or from West, from North or from South, nor do the clouds pour their rain into it, but only the fresh spring at the bottom wells up and completely suffuses, pervades, fills, and permeates it, so that not the smallest part of the lake is left unsaturated with fresh water, even so the monk . . . permeates his body with pleasure and joy arising from concentration. . .

As in a lake with lotus plants some lotus flowers are born in the water, develop in the water, remain below the surface of the water, and draw their nourishment from the depths of the water, and their blooms and roots are suffused, pervaded, filled, and permeated with fresh water, so that not the smallest part of any lotus flower is left unpermeated with fresh water, even so the monk . . . permeates his body with pleasure without joy . . .

As a man might cloak himself from head to foot in a white mantle, so that not the smallest part of his body was left uncovered by the white mantle, even so the monk sits having covered his body with a state of extreme equanimity and concentration . . . *Digha Nikaya XI, 82*

Sore knees, a stiff neck, long periods filled with day dreams; thoughts, memories, and anxious mental wanderings, such is the stuff that meditations are sometimes made on. To begin with, at least. Meditation is not easy. It requires energy and determination. Anyone who has taken up the practice will be familiar with those sessions when they struggle almost fruitlessly just to stay awake, just to keep with the technique for a few minutes, or for a few moments on end!

Of course, even when our meditation practice seems to be going badly it has some value. It is at least a break from the usual hurly-burly — a change that can be as good as a rest. All those wanderings and fantasies can have some therapeutic effect, allowing our minds to go 'off-line' and unravel a bit. And the humiliation of having to admit to ourselves that our minds are almost out of control can have a positive, chastening effect. In the face of repeated failure we come to realize that we must take ourselves in hand, that we are not as clear and sorted out as we like to think. Thus our meditation practice can become a useful guide as we try to establish a more ethical basis to our lives.

But meditation practice is not always like that. It certainly doesn't have to be. If we keep our determination strong, and bring forth the necessary effort, we can find ourselves having some very different experiences indeed. At times we feel physical tensions magically dropping away, leaving us with an all-pervading sense of relaxation and peace. An anxious whining in our minds subsides and ceases; suddenly we find ourselves quiet, as though a noise of which we were previously unaware had just stopped, leaving us calmly sitting there, fully awake, fully alert, fully in tune with our practice. Sometimes a heated flow of angry or resentful memories is transmuted into a radiant force of pure energy; we feel filled with new strength, vigour, and brightness.

As we conquer the hindrances, the object of our practice — be it our breathing, a feeling of loving kindness, or a visualized *bodhisattva* form — which we have been hunting and chasing around the periphery of our minds, moves clearly into the centre of our awareness, *becomes* the centre of our awareness, and all the other elements of our consciousness fall into place and rearrange themselves around it. Now, rather than obstructing our practice, they are complementing, strengthening, and refining it. We experience a tremendous thrill of freedom from conflict and distraction, and a simple sense of sufficiency and dignity arises.

This kind of experience may last for minutes on end, or for just a few moments. It might be quite subtle, like a new flavouring to the practice, or it may be so powerful, so exhilarating and blissful that the hairs of our head literally stand on end.

What has happened is that our meditation practice has allowed us, first of all, to bring all the elements of our ordinary everyday consciousness into harmony; and now it is taking us further. The factors and forces of our unconscious heights and depths, attracted by the power of our concentrated state, are beginning to get involved as well. Thus we enter the *jhanas* (Sanskrit:*dhyana*) of *samatha* meditation.

Meditation has, in the Buddhist tradition, two major aspects. The highest aspect, the ultimate goal of meditation practice, is *vipassana*, or Insight into the Unconditioned. Such Insight may arise spontaneously, as a reflex of the interplay between our meditation and our everyday life, or it might 'arise' (Insight into the Transcendental cannot be forced or 'made to happen') in the context of a specific Insight meditation technique, such as the Contemplation of the Six Elements, or the Contemplation of Impermanence.

In its *samatha* aspect meditation has the aim of stopping and calming the habitual, reactive process of the lower consciousness, as well as of invigorating and enriching it. The jhana states are therefore our goal when we embark upon the practice of techniques like the Mindfulness of Breathing and the *metta bhavana*.

According to Buddhist teaching, eight jhanas, or categories of meditative absorption, can be identified along what is, in fact, a scale of uninterrupted increase in concentration and mental refinement. The Buddha not only defined the psychological constituents of each stage but, perhaps to make the teaching even more accessible, also gave a set of images that evoke the qualities of the first four. The second set of four, known as the *arupa jhanas*, the 'formless jhanas', with names like 'the sphere of no-thingness', and 'the sphere of neither-perception-nor-non-perception', cannot, perhaps, even be evoked in images.

It is worth briefly considering each of the Buddha's similes. Just as it is valuable to be able to identify each of the hindrances that we encounter, so too is it worthwhile to have a feeling at least for the manifestations of success that our efforts will bring forth.

As a simile for the first jhana, the Buddha offered the image of a perfect mixture of soap powder and water (soap powder has been made in India for thousands of years from the grated fruit of a tree). The soap and water are so mixed that not a grain of powder is left unsaturated, while not a droplet of water is left over.

Just a little reflection will suggest that this is an image which evokes the resolution of opposites. The powder is dry; the water is wet. The two elements have been brought into perfect union, providing us with an image of unification, integration, and balance. Such is the first jhana: a state in which we feel no conflict, no resistance, no contrary pulls, and experience no irrelevant mental activity: a state of peaceful, radiant calm and poise.

This state of mind, however, is not to be regarded as something far off or ethereally remote. It is quite easily within reach of anyone who meditates regularly and sincerely. According to the Venerable Sangharakshita it is, in fact, the state in which we should aim to live all the time: a happy, healthy, human state of mind.

For the second jhana, the Buddha gave the simile of a subterranean spring bubbling up into a deep, cool pond. The suggestion here is that the concentrated, unified consciousness of the first jhana is being fed by something from an even higher — or deeper — level of consciousness. This stage has been called the stage of 'inspiration' since it is analogous to the state talked of by creative artists. New richness, new potency, new life erupts, or flows into the mind, as if from outside. The forces that 'flow in' are in fact aspects of our own unconscious heights and depths, but because they are beyond our normal experience, coming from outside our conscious personality, we may even have the impression that they are coming *literally* from outside. Perhaps because this sense of inspiration can actually manifest in visionary or even verbal 'prophetic' terms, it is possible to believe that we are receiving messages from a muse, or a god, or from the angels, when the truth is that we are being enriched by our own deeper and finer aspects.

A lotus flower, floating just on the surface of a lake, is the simile for the third jhana, which Sangarakshita has called the stage of 'permeation'. Whereas in the second jhana the higher consciousness seemed to be flowing into *us, now, in the third jhana, we are in it.* We are suffused by it, saturated by it, having our whole being in it. There is no longer any feeling of separation between us and the state of bright illumined consciousness. In feeling at least, in terms of immediate experience at least, as distinct from the terms of Insight and any permanent transformation, we are experiencing an attenuation of the subject-object dichotomy, even a momentary dissolution of it. For this reason the third jhana can be called the 'mystical' stage.

Finally, for the fourth jhana, we have the image of a man who has taken a cool bath on a hot day, and now sits completely enfolded in a pure white robe. Here the water symbolism has been left behind; it has been transcended. The higher state of consciousness has become so strong, so powerful, that it becomes almost tangible. Not only does it protect us from all negative influences, but it can actually take a kind of offensive against them. In the fourth jhana various supernormal powers, such as clairvoyance, clairaudience, and healing become possible.

It is not easy to grasp these states of mind with our imagination. The images can only serve to evoke some feeling for them. After all, once the first jhana has been left behind, and as we progress through the jhanas, thought too is left behind, and our experience has less and less to do with the sensuous plane of experience — and therefore with words and even images. But it should at least be clear by now that meditation can lead us into some very powerful and creative mental states. There is nothing passive or soporific about it!

Of course these states can only be of a temporary nature, briefly sustained by our efforts in meditation. They guarantee no permanent transformation or contact with the Transcendental. Only Insight will do that. But regular experience of jhana states is extraordinarily refreshing and energizing. It connects us with the sources of vitality and creativity. Further, it serves to weaken the hold that our negative, self-centred attitudes and habitual reactions have on us. Thus we create the basis for Insight to arise, and a receptive base for it.

But there is another vital aspect to jhana experience.

Sangharakshita has said, 'A jhana is not a "state" in which "we" are, but a way in which we reorganize our being.' (*Peace is a Fire*, Windhorse Publications). The jhana state is not something which gets added onto our ordinary, unchanged selves. Rather, the jhana state is an experience of ourselves as we reorganize, sublimate, and refine the various factors of our mundane (as opposed to Transcendental) consciousness. The jhana states are our experience of ourselves as we potentially exist, on higher and higher planes of being.

As human beings we have the possibility of living at different levels. We may well be familiar with those times when we live at a less than human level: when we are in the grip of craving or hatred, when we sink into an animal torpor, or when we wander aimlessly about, living on but the most superficial level. We can also think of those times when we are more completely and truly human, when we are self-aware, acting responsibly, non-neurotic, and directed.

Through meditation practice we get the opportunity to live on higher levels still. As we strengthen our experience of the jhana states we actually begin to live out some of these higher possibilities: we *become* gods — *devas* — radiant beings feeding on joy.

As we become more familiar with these states we will become more confidently aware of our multi-dimensionality. We come to realize that we have some measure of choice as to the level of being at which we live. At the end of the Path, beyond those flashes of Insight, awaits the Transcendental: Buddhahood. But long before then, right now, today, as we take our seats for a period of meditation, we can enrich and glorify our lives by existing, if only for a moment or two, or for a few minutes, as beings of light.

MEDITATION AND ACTION
By Dharmachari Subhuti

Life sometimes seems to consist of nothing but irreconcilable opposites. Again and again we are faced with the impossibility of uniting in a single moment all the contradictory forces of our nature. Masculine and feminine, head and heart, introversion and extroversion: each psychic pole is seemingly exclusive of the other and we are often caught by the demands of our circumstances in the wrong polarity at the wrong time.

One of the hardest of these oppositions to bring into harmony is that between the demands and attractions of the inner and outer worlds. Each is, in its own way, rich and enticing, offering its own fascinations and allurements. The world around is so complex and multiform, defying generalization in its dizzying array. The world within promises new vistas of freedom, fresh springs of vitality, dazzling insights and pure feeling. So often we find it hard to balance these two so that we are able to gain the fulfilment and self-knowledge which action brings, together with the clarity and wholeness which come from meditation. Frequently, we spend our time reacting between a frenzied and somewhat superficial activity and a defensive, rather precious isolation. This constant oscillation between the extroverted and the introverted poles is a symptom of our lack of integration and true individuality. We have not grasped our lives and made of the different forces seething within our breasts a satisfying unity, like the different notes in a musical scale threaded together by a single melody. Jangling discordantly, we stagger from activity to meditation and back, without much conscious control.

In the teaching of the Five Spiritual Faculties we are shown that the harmonizing of these various polarities — Meditation and Vigour (or introversion and extroversion), Faith and Wisdom (or emotion and reason) — is the task of Mindfulness. What this means, in the first place, is that we must take responsibility for our lives. This has been spoken of as 'keeping the initiative with our lives', making sure that we do not become the passive victims of our lives and that we do not respond like mere puppets to the pushes and pulls of the daily round. We must seize the reins, take the driver's seat, and live our lives for ourselves.

The Pali word *sati* which is usually translated as 'Mindfulness', includes in its meaning both memory and forethought. To be mindful means to remember, in the sense of our learning from our past experience. Forethought involves seeing the implications of our actions, seeing as far as we can what we are letting ourselves in for when we commence any act. In this case, it involves being aware of the need to keep meditation and action in balance by seeing what is happening in the present, what has gone wrong in the past, and where our future actions are leading us.

If we apply mindfulness in this way we will be better able to bring meditation and action into dialectical harmony. Probably, for most people, this will involve periods of intensive activity followed by periods of intensive meditation. The interval between each phase and the distance between the extremes will vary from person to person. Some prefer to work very hard for periods of time — six months, a year, even longer — keeping up only a basic daily practice of meditation for a while; then they will spend a month or more in solitary retreat or at a meditation centre like Vajraloka. Others like to keep more of an equilibrium within each day. Yet others choose to do long periods of constant meditation with occasional forays into the world of action.

The variation is determined by temperament, circumstance, and spiritual maturity. It is a matter of honesty and mindfulness to determine which pattern suits one best and helps one to integrate and harmonize the full range of one's potentiality. Within the context of one's overall commitment and particular responsibilities and of one's fellowship with others in the spiritual community, one should be aware of this steady pendulum swing from pole to pole. The swing should be taken into account when one takes up one's duties.

If the individual achieves in his own life a unique and natural blending of meditation and action they will become for him the means of steady progress relatively free from inner conflict. He will know both the joy of action and the delight of meditation.

Action well done brings its own special joys. There is the satisfaction of achieving what we set out to do, of using and testing muscle and brain, heart and hand. In acting we bring forward powers we never knew we had; we are asked for determination, courage, and cunning hitherto dormant within us. Action stretches and extends us, shows up our weaknesses and strengths. Action, properly directed, demands that we go beyond ourselves and that we reach new levels of energy and integration. Above all, action is objective. It puts us into the arena of the world which reveals us because it resists us. In every thought, word, and deed we make ourselves known to ourselves as we imprint ourselves upon the opaque surface of the external world.

The feature of the world which most eludes our control is other people. However much we want them to, they will not easily dance to our tune. Matter we can force to our shaping — we can mould clay, bend metal — but we cannot easily shape other people to our will. In acting *with* and *for* others we are brought most squarely up against ourselves.

How much do we really care about them? To what extent
are we willing to consider their needs before our own? Our
inspiration and our metta receive their greatest testing in
our work with others. We should not over-stress the benefits
of action to the agent. Surely, the crucial point about action
is that it contributes to the welfare of the world. The world
so badly needs the efforts of those with skilful motivation
and it so badly needs the Dharma. Skilful action is needed.

Meditation, on the other hand, brings us into contact with
ourselves on new heights. When we break through into real
meditation we experience ourselves as more than mortal
clay. We find that we are, as it were, spiritual beings existing
in a dimension of hitherto unimagined clarity and brilliance.
We discover that we have a destiny which far transcends
our earthly career. We have access to inspiration and delight
which spring up endlessly within us. No longer are we the
victims of conflict and contradiction but we feel unified and
purposeful, in touch with our own significance and
meaning. We feel fulfilled and contained, contented and
unsullied. Of course, the ultimate benefit of meditation is
that it provides the basis for Insight. Through our practice
of meditation we can systematically direct ourselves to
seeing things as they really are.

Each of these, action and meditation, has its own
attractions and benefits. Why then do we oscillate between
the two? The point is that we cannot sustain ourselves
satisfactorily in either mode without some experience of the
other. Action without meditation leads to our becoming lost
in mere activity. We lose all perspective and, however noble
our original purpose, find ourselves working for baser and
baser motives with less and less vision and inspiration. We
forget who we are, identifying ourselves more and more
with the details of our activity and less and less with its
overall purpose and meaning. The light goes out of our eyes
and we become either dull and listless or else hard and
unpleasantly aggressive. All our noble ideals are lost and

we do not benefit others.

Meditation without action eventually leads to loss of energy. Many people know themselves so little that without doing something concrete they cannot properly experience themselves. Meditation is too refined, too immaterial to be sustained for long unless one has already to some degree unified and purified one's energies. Restlessness and boredom set in and day-dreams and fantasies possess the mind.

And so we swing between action and meditation: acting until we begin to lose contact with our inspiration and purpose, meditating until we cannot sustain the pure flow of meditative states and find that we must engage ourselves in action once more.

So far I have talked of meditation and action as if they were two mutually exclusive conditions. Clearly, they need not be and should not be. It is possible to act from a state of concentration and clarity. It is possible to retain at all times a sense of higher purpose and meaning, to feel fully engaged and yet constantly refreshed and invigorated. In other words, our action can be the expression of a higher state of consciousness.

On the other hand, meditation is itself a form of action. When we are meditating we are making an effort and we are moving forward to ever higher levels of consciousness. Not only that, but in the higher reaches of meditation our own very positive state begins to radiate from us and to have an experienceable effect on those around us. When we look closely, the line between meditation and action wears a little thin. Indeed, it is only a reflection of our relative spiritual immaturity that we experience a tension between the two at all. We do not have sufficient vision to act consistently from inspiration and we do not have sufficient purity of energy to be able to be consistently effective in meditation. So, while we must try to unify the two at all times, we must constantly redress imbalance as it develops by giving special attention to one or other as the need arises. While we are acting, we must try to remain in as positive a mental state as we can and when we are meditating we must try to remain as energetic and alive as we can. When our actions become more and more superficial in motivation then we must strengthen our contact with the depths of meditation. When meditation becomes hard to sustain for lack of vitality then we need the invigoration of action. Constant mindfulness will teach us how to blend the two in our lives so that we remain in as positive and effective a condition as possible at all times.

But in the end we must break through that distinction altogether. Our action must become so complete that it is the perfect expression of the highest mental clarity. Our meditation must be so powerful that it lifts all who are open to it beyond themselves. Action and meditation, meditation and action, are unified here in the life of the Bodhisattva. At rest he is meditating: his meditation is the radiation of compassion to all that lives. At play he is engaged in compassionate activity which is never separated from the bliss and wisdom of meditation. In him, all contradictions are resolved and transcended and he has become a flood of pure feeling for living beings, acting tirelessly for their welfare.

This unification of action and meditation is expressed iconographically in the figures of many Bodhisattvas who sit with the left leg drawn up in meditation and the right stepping down compassionately into the world of suffering. Yet though they step down they never leave their transcendental seat. They see the world with all its frustrations, imperfections, and sufferings — yet they know that it is not really so. Though they enter joyfully into action in the world they remain in the core of their being untouched by it.

So meditation and action are, at the outset, but the jarring contradictory demands of the inner and outer worlds. With mindfulness, we weave them into our lives so that they work with and for each other. Deeper still, the tension lessens and we experience more and more of one within the other. Ultimately, with Transcendental Insight, we break the boundaries altogether and meditation becomes action, action becomes meditation, inner and outer worlds merge into a single whole.